The First Book of Enoch

The Lost Ancient Scripture of Angels, Giants, and the End Times

A Modern Translation

Adapted for the Contemporary Reader

Enoch the Patriarch

Translated by Tim Zengerink

Table Of Contents

Preface - Message to the Reader

What If You Could Help Rebuild the Greatest Library in Human History?

Thousands of years ago, the Library of Alexandria stood as the crown jewel of human achievement — a sanctuary where the collected wisdom of every known civilization was gathered, preserved, and shared freely.

And then, it was lost.

Through fire, conquest, and the slow erosion of time, humanity lost not just books — but ideas, dreams, discoveries, and stories that could have changed the world forever.

Today, the Library of Alexandria lives again — and you are invited to be a part of its restoration.

Our mission is simple yet profound:

To rebuild the greatest library the world has ever known, and to translate all timeless works into every language and dialect, so that no seeker of knowledge is ever left behind again.

By joining our movement to rebuild the modern Library of Alexandria, you become part of an unprecedented mission:

- **Unlimited Access to the Greatest Audiobooks & eBooks Ever Written:**

  Instantly explore thousands of legendary works—Plato, Shakespeare, Jane Austen, Leo Tolstoy, and countless more. All instantly available to read or listen, placing a complete literary universe at your fingertips.

- **Beautiful Paperback & Deluxe Editions at Printing Cost**

  Own any title as an elegant paperback, deluxe hardcover, or stunning collectible boxset—offered to you at true printing cost, delivered straight to your door. Build your personal Library of Alexandria, crafted for beauty, built for durability, and worthy of proud display.

- **Fresh Translations for Modern Readers—in Every Language & Dialect**

  Enjoy timeless masterpieces reimagined in clear, contemporary language—no more outdated phrases or obscure references. Alongside the original versions, we're tirelessly translating these classics into every language and dialect imaginable, ensuring accessibility and understanding across cultures and generations.

- **Join a Global Renaissance of Literature & Knowledge**

  You directly support expanding our library, publishing deluxe editions at true cost, translating works into all global languages, and bringing humanity's greatest stories to people everywhere. By joining today, you're not just preserving a legacy of masterpieces; you set in motion a powerful wave of literary accessibility.

Become a Torchbearer of Knowledge.

Join us for free now at **LibraryofAlexandria.com**

Together, we will ensure that the light of human wisdom never fades again.

With gratitude and a shared love of knowledge,

The Modern Library of Alexandria Team

Visit:

www.libraryofalexandria.com

Or scan the code below:

Introduction

Across the sands of history, certain texts have profoundly impacted the spiritual imagination and religious traditions of humanity. Among these rare writings stands prominently The First Book of Enoch, also known as Enoch I—a captivating narrative steeped in myth, prophecy, and profound theological significance. Often termed a "lost book" or "hidden scripture," its intriguing content has fascinated theologians, historians, and seekers of ancient wisdom for centuries.

Attributed to Enoch, the seventh patriarch after Adam, whose life is briefly mentioned in the Book of Genesis, Enoch occupies a unique position. According to scriptural tradition, he did not die but was "taken up" by God, leaving behind an enigmatic legacy. Genesis 5:24 succinctly states, "Enoch walked with God; then he was no more, because God took him." This mysterious figure, whose life bridged heaven and earth, offers profound insights into the nature of divine-human interactions, celestial realms, and apocalyptic visions.

The First Book of Enoch is a foundational text of apocalyptic literature, originating from the ancient

Jewish tradition between approximately 300 BCE and the 1st century CE. Discovered among the Dead Sea Scrolls at Qumran, fragments of Enochic texts were carefully preserved by the Essenes, an ascetic Jewish community. The most complete version survives today in the Ethiopic language, as a central text within the Ethiopian Orthodox Church's biblical canon.

Though widely known in antiquity, The Book of Enoch gradually fell out of favor with mainstream Judaism and was largely excluded from later Jewish scripture collections and canonical Christian texts. Nonetheless, it profoundly influenced early Christian theology, especially regarding angelology, demonology, and eschatology. It is explicitly referenced in the New Testament Book of Jude (1:14-15), attesting to its significance within early Christian communities.

Today, The First Book of Enoch is experiencing a remarkable resurgence of interest. Modern readers, seeking spiritual depth beyond conventional scriptures, find within its pages compelling narratives of celestial beings, fallen angels, giants, prophetic revelations, and visions of cosmic conflict. Its renewed appeal lies in its ability to illuminate timeless questions: Who are we? Why is the world marked by conflict between good and evil? What is humanity's destiny?

Major Themes

1. The Watchers and Their Fall

Central to Enoch's narrative is the detailed account of the "Watchers"—angelic beings who descend to Earth, driven by forbidden desires. Their rebellion against divine command, and subsequent interaction with humanity, brings forth catastrophic consequences. These accounts explore the origins of evil, the nature of sin, and divine justice, themes echoed throughout later religious texts.

2. The Book of Heavenly Secrets

Enoch's heavenly journeys offer astonishing glimpses into celestial mysteries, cosmological truths, and divine secrets revealed by angelic guides. These visionary experiences depict a structured cosmos governed by divine law, presenting the universe as an intricate tapestry woven by a purposeful divine design.

3. The Prophecies of Judgment

Apocalyptic visions form a significant portion of Enoch's prophecies, vividly portraying the ultimate triumph of divine justice. Enoch foresees a final judgment, where the forces of darkness and corruption are decisively overcome by the righteous governance of the divine. This powerful imagery profoundly influenced later apocalyptic literature, including the Book of Revelation.

4. Themes of Redemption and Restoration

Amidst the dramatic visions of conflict and judgment, Enoch also presents deeply hopeful themes of redemption. Humanity, despite its fallibility and vulnerability to temptation, is depicted as central to the divine plan for cosmic restoration. These themes resonate powerfully with modern readers searching for spiritual renewal and deeper existential meaning.

Why This Modern Translation Matters

This carefully adapted modern translation seeks to preserve the profound depth of the original texts while rendering the language accessible and engaging for contemporary readers. It captures the essence and intensity of Enoch's original visions, allowing the narrative's wisdom and theological insights to speak clearly to today's spiritual seekers. The adapted language removes barriers, enabling a wider audience to appreciate and deeply engage with this ancient text.

Understanding Celestial Conflict

The First Book of Enoch uniquely highlights the unseen spiritual warfare between celestial beings, elucidating concepts of angelic rebellion, demonic forces, and spiritual realms. Its detailed descriptions of angelic hierarchies and spiritual entities provide valuable context for understanding the religious and cultural milieu from which subsequent theological traditions emerged.

Enoch's visions emphasize humanity's critical role in the unfolding cosmic drama, situating human experience within a much broader spiritual and cosmic context. These perspectives encourage readers to reflect deeply on humanity's purpose, ethical responsibilities, and ultimate destiny. The text's powerful exploration of redemption invites individuals to ponder their own spiritual journeys and the collective path toward renewal and harmony.

As you embark upon this literary and spiritual journey, consider yourself a participant in an ancient conversation—a timeless dialogue bridging millennia. The First Book of Enoch offers you more than mere historical intrigue; it presents an opportunity to engage deeply with ancient wisdom, challenge modern assumptions, and explore profound truths that continue to shape humanity's spiritual landscape.

This book invites you to uncover the mysteries of the divine realm, contemplate the eternal struggle between good and evil, and reflect on the ultimate meaning of existence itself. May this reading illuminate your understanding, inspire your spirit, and enrich your exploration of the mysteries that continue to captivate the human heart.

Now, step into the ancient world, explore its celestial secrets, and let the profound revelations of Enoch guide you toward deeper understanding and spiritual enlightenment.

The First Book of Enoch

Chapter I

Enoch's words of blessing were given to those who are chosen and live rightly. He spoke to those who will be alive during a time of great trouble when all the wicked and godless will be removed.

Enoch, a righteous man, received a vision from God. His eyes were opened, and he saw the Holy One in the heavens. The angels showed him this vision, and he came to understand everything they revealed. But this message was not meant for his own time—it was for a future generation.

He spoke about those who were chosen and delivered this message:

The Great and Holy One will leave His dwelling place.
The eternal God will come down to the earth, even to Mount Sinai.
He will step out from His camp
And show His great power from the highest heavens.

People everywhere will be filled with fear,
And even the Watchers—mighty beings—will
    tremble.
Terror will spread across the whole world.

The strongest mountains will shake,
And high hills will be flattened.

They will melt like wax in a blazing fire.
The earth itself will crack apart,
And everything on it will be destroyed.
A great judgment will come upon all people.

But those who live rightly will have peace.
God will protect the ones He has chosen,
And His kindness will surround them.

They will belong to Him completely,
And they will thrive.
They will receive His blessing,
And He will care for each one of them.
His light will shine on them,
And He will fill them with peace.

And look—He will come with tens of thousands of
    His holy ones
To bring justice to all people,

To remove the wicked,
And to judge everyone for their ungodly actions
And the harsh words they have spoken against Him.

Chapter II

Look up at the sky and see how everything moves in order. The stars and other lights follow their paths, rising and setting at the right times. They never change the pattern set for them.

Now look at the earth and notice everything that happens from one end to the other. The land stays firm and steady, never changing. Everything on it continues as it has been, showing the work of God for all to see.

Think about the seasons—summer and winter. See how the earth is covered with water, and how the clouds, dew, and rain settle over the land.

Chapter III

During winter, most trees look dried up and lose all their leaves. But there are fourteen kinds of trees that don't do this. Instead of shedding their leaves, they hold onto them for two to three years until fresh ones grow.

Chapter IV

Watch how the sun sits high in the sky during summer, shining straight down on the land. The heat is so strong that you look for shade to cool off. Even the ground and rocks get so hot that walking on them becomes impossible.

Chapter V

Notice how trees grow fresh green leaves and bear fruit. Pay attention to the world around you and see that the One who lives forever has created everything this way. His works continue in the same cycle, year after year, just as He intended. Everything follows His plan, and nothing changes from what He has commanded.

Look at the seas and rivers too. They follow their course exactly as He directed, never straying from His orders.

But you have not remained faithful. You have not followed the Lord's commands. Instead, you have turned away and spoken with pride, using harsh words against Him. Because of your stubbornness and hardened hearts, you will not find peace.

As a result, you will regret your days, and your years will end in disaster. Your suffering will grow, leading to eternal punishment with no mercy.

During that time, your names will be used as a lasting curse by those who do what is right. People will use your name when they wish harm upon others, and sinners and those without faith will be condemned just as you are. For those who reject God, only a curse remains.

But those who are righteous will be filled with joy. Their sins will be forgiven, and they will receive mercy, peace, and patience. Salvation will come to them, bringing light and hope.

For sinners, there will be no salvation—only a curse. But for the chosen ones, there will be light, happiness, and peace. They will inherit the earth.

Wisdom will be given to them, and they will live without sin. They will not fall into arrogance or wrongdoing, and those who are wise will remain humble.

They will not turn away from what is right, nor will they sin again. They will not die as a result of judgment or anger. Instead, they will live full and peaceful lives, filled with joy. Their happiness will continue forever, and they will enjoy true peace for all their days.

Chapter VI

As people on Earth grew in number, they had daughters who were beautiful. The angels, who came from heaven, saw them and wanted to be with them. They said to each other, "Let's choose wives from among these women and have children with them."

Their leader, Semjâzâ, was unsure and said, "I'm afraid you won't all go through with this plan, and I'll be the only one punished for committing such a great sin." But the others reassured him, saying, "Let's all make a promise together and swear an oath. We will not abandon this plan but will see it through."

So they all swore an oath and made a binding agreement to carry it out. There were two hundred of them in total, and during the time of Jared, they came down to the top of Mount Hermon. They named it Mount Hermon because it was the place where they made their oath and sealed it with a curse.

These were their leaders: Semjâzâ, their chief, along with Arâkîba, Râmêêl, Kôkabîêl, Tâmîêl, Râmîêl, Dânêl, Êzêqêêl, Barâqîjâl, Asâêl, Armârôs, Batârêl, Anânêl, Zaqîêl, Samsâpêêl, Satarêl, Tûrêl, Jômjâêl, and Sariêl. Each of them led a group of ten.

Chapter VII

The others also took wives for themselves, each choosing one. They lived with them and corrupted themselves. They taught the women magical spells, charms, and how to use roots and different plants.

The women became pregnant and gave birth to gigantic children, growing to an unbelievable height. These giants ate everything that people had worked hard to produce. When there was no longer enough food, they turned on the humans and started to eat them instead.

The giants also committed terrible acts against birds, animals, reptiles, and fish. They even began to eat each other's flesh and drink blood. Because of their wickedness, the earth cried out against them.

Chapter VIII

Azâzêl taught people how to make weapons like swords, knives, shields, and armor. He showed them how to work with metals found in the earth. He also introduced jewelry-making, the use of antimony for makeup, and ways to make the eyes look more attractive. He revealed the secrets of precious stones and different colorful dyes.

Because of this, people became more wicked. They fell into immorality, were deceived, and grew more corrupt in their ways. Semjâzâ taught them spells and how to use plant roots for magic. Armârôs showed them how to break enchantments. Barâqîjâl taught astrology, while Kôkabêl revealed the mysteries of the stars. Ezêqêêl explained how to read cloud patterns, Araqiêl taught the signs of the earth, Shamsiêl revealed the secrets of the sun, and Sariêl explained how the moon moves.

As people suffered and died, their cries of pain reached up to heaven.

Chapter IX

Michael, Uriel, Raphael, and Gabriel looked down from heaven and saw that the earth was filled with violence and wrongdoing. They said to each other, "The earth, which was meant to be a peaceful place, is now crying out because of the suffering, and its cries have reached the gates of heaven.

The souls of people are begging us, the holy ones in heaven, to bring their case before the Most High."

Then they spoke to the Lord, saying, "Mighty God, King of kings, ruler over all things, Your throne has stood for all time, and Your name is holy, glorious, and blessed forever.

You created everything, and You have power over all things. Nothing is hidden from You—everything is clear before Your eyes.

You see what Azâzêl has done. He has taught people evil ways and revealed secrets that were meant to stay in heaven—things humans were never supposed to know.

And Semjâzâ, whom You put in charge of his followers, has come down to the earth and taken human women as his own. He and his companions have sinned with them and taught them sinful ways.

Now, their children, the giants, have brought destruction, and the earth is filled with violence and corruption because of them.

The souls of those who have died are crying out for justice, and their voices have reached heaven. Their sorrow will not stop because of all the wickedness happening on earth.

Lord, You knew all of this before it happened. You see what is going on, yet You have not told us what we should do about it."

Chapter X

Then the Most High, the Holy and Great One, spoke and sent Uriel to Lamech's son. He told him, "Go to

Noah and warn him in My name. Tell him to hide himself and reveal to him what is about to happen. A great flood will soon cover the earth and destroy everything. Tell him how to survive so that he and his descendants can continue for all generations."

Then the Lord spoke to Raphael, saying, "Capture Azâzêl, tie him up, and throw him into the darkness. Dig a deep pit in the desert of Dûdâêl and cast him into it. Cover him with sharp, jagged rocks and block out all light so that he never sees it again. He will remain there forever. On the day of the final judgment, he will be thrown into the fire. Heal the earth from the corruption caused by the fallen angels so that the plague they brought may end. This way, humanity will not be destroyed because of the forbidden knowledge the Watchers have shared. The whole earth has been ruined by the things Azâzêl has taught, so place all the blame for sin on him."

Then the Lord said to Gabriel, "Go after the evil ones and those born from forbidden unions. Destroy the children of the fallen angels and make them fight each other until they wipe themselves out. They will not live long lives. If their fathers plead for them, do not listen, for they believe they will live forever and expect to reach five hundred years."

The Lord then spoke to Michael, saying, "Go and capture Semjâzâ and his followers, who have taken human women and made themselves unclean with them."

Once their sons have destroyed one another, and they have watched their loved ones perish, bind them for seventy generations deep within the earth. Keep them there until the final judgment, when they will be condemned forever. At that time, they will be cast into the fiery abyss, suffering in a prison where they will be locked away for eternity. Those who are sentenced to destruction will remain with them until the end of all generations.

Wipe out the spirits of the wicked and the children of the fallen angels, for they have harmed humanity. Remove all sin from the earth and put an end to evil. Let righteousness and truth take root and grow. It will bring blessings, and goodness will remain forever in joy and peace.

Then the righteous will be saved. They will live long lives, having thousands of children, and will enjoy both their youth and old age in peace.

After that, the whole earth will be restored to goodness. It will be covered with trees and filled with blessings. Every kind of tree will grow, and vineyards will be planted, producing an abundance of grapes.

Crops will yield a thousand times more than before, and olive trees will produce ten times more oil.

Cleanse the world of all oppression, wickedness, and sin. Remove every trace of evil, wiping it completely from the earth.

All people will become righteous, and every nation will give Me honor and praise. They will worship Me together. The earth will be purified from all corruption, sin, and suffering, and I will never again bring such destruction upon it. From generation to generation, the world will remain in peace for all eternity.

Chapter XI

In those days, I will open the great storehouses of blessings in heaven and pour them down onto the earth. These blessings will flow generously, rewarding the hard work of people and enriching their lives. They will not only nourish the land but also bring renewal and prosperity to everyone, filling all of creation with abundance.

Truth and peace will come together in perfect harmony, lasting through every generation. They will be the foundation of life, ensuring that goodness and balance remain forever. This lasting bond between truth and peace will create a world where righteousness thrives, guiding and giving hope to humanity for all time.

Chapter XII

I, Enoch, was giving blessings and praise to the Lord of majesty, the King of all time. As I was doing this, the Watchers called out to me. They spoke to me as Enoch the scribe and said, "Enoch, writer of righteousness, go and deliver a message to the Watchers of heaven—those who left their high and holy home. They have made themselves unclean by taking human wives and acting like the people of the earth.

Tell them, 'You have brought great destruction upon the world. Because of this, you will never find peace, and your sins will never be forgiven. Since you take joy in your children, you will have to watch them die and be destroyed. You will grieve for them and cry out forever, but know this—you will never receive mercy or peace.'"

Chapter XIII

Enoch went to Azâzêl and said, "You will never have peace. A severe judgment has been given against you, and you will be chained. You will not be shown mercy or have your requests granted because of the evil you have taught and the sinful acts you have led people to commit."

Then I went to speak to all of them together, and they were overcome with fear. They trembled in terror and begged me to write a petition for them, hoping they could be forgiven. They wanted me to bring their request before the Lord of heaven.

From that moment, they could no longer speak with Him or even look up toward heaven because they were ashamed of their sins and the punishment they had received. I wrote down their petition, including their prayer about their spirits, their actions, and their plea for forgiveness and a longer life.

I went to sit by the waters of Dan, in the land of Dan, southwest of Mount Hermon. There, I read their petition over and over until I fell asleep.

As I slept, I had a dream and saw visions. I saw punishments being carried out, and a voice called out, telling me to deliver a message to the fallen angels and warn them.

When I woke up, I went to them. They were gathered together, weeping in Abelsjâîl, a place between Lebanon and Sênêsêr. Their faces were filled with shame.

I told them everything I had seen in my dream. Then, I began to speak words of truth and righteousness and rebuked the fallen Watchers for their sins.

Chapter XIV

This book contains words of truth and a warning to the fallen Watchers, as commanded by the Holy Great One in a vision.

While I was asleep, I saw something that I will now share, using the voice and breath given to me by the Great One. He has gifted humanity with speech and understanding so that we can think and communicate. Just as He has given people wisdom, He has also given me the duty to warn the Watchers, the heavenly beings who turned away.

I wrote down your request, but in my vision, I saw that it will not be accepted. Judgment has already been decided, and your plea will never be granted, not now or ever. From this moment on, you will never return to heaven. The decision is final, and you will remain bound to the earth for all time.

You will watch as your beloved sons are destroyed, and there will be no joy left for you. They will die by the sword before your eyes, and your prayers for them will not be heard. Even if you cry out, pray, and repeat every word written in your request, it will not be answered.

Then, in my vision, I saw something incredible: Clouds gathered around me and called me forward, while mist surrounded me. Bright stars and flashes of lightning moved quickly, and powerful winds lifted me, carrying me high into the heavens.

I traveled until I reached a massive crystal wall, surrounded by flames of fire. The sight filled me with fear. I passed through the fire and saw a magnificent house made entirely of crystal. Its walls sparkled like gems, and its foundation was also crystal-clear.

The ceiling of this house looked like the sky filled with stars and lightning, and fiery beings moved between them. The heavens above were as clear as water. A blazing fire surrounded the walls, and the gates of the house glowed with flames.

When I entered, I felt an intense heat, like fire, and at the same time, a deep cold, like ice. There was no comfort inside—only a powerful sense of fear. I trembled and fell on my face.

As I lay there, another vision appeared before me: A second house, even greater and more magnificent than the first, stood open before me. This house was built entirely of fire, and its beauty and size were beyond anything I could describe.

The floor was made of fire, and above it stretched paths of lightning and stars. The ceiling burned with flames. Inside, I saw a high throne that shone like crystal, with wheels as bright as the sun. Around it were visions of heavenly beings.

Beneath the throne, streams of flaming fire flowed so brightly that I could not look at them directly. Seated on the throne was the Great Glory. His robe was brighter than the sun and whiter than any snow. No angel could approach Him because of His overwhelming majesty and brilliance. No living being could look upon His face.

Flames of fire surrounded Him, and a great fire burned before Him. No one could get near Him. Tens of thousands upon thousands stood before Him, yet He needed no advice from anyone. The holiest ones in His presence never left His side, not during the day or the night.

I lay there, trembling, with my face pressed to the ground. Then the Lord Himself spoke, calling my name, "Come here, Enoch, and listen to My words."

One of the holy ones came to me, helped me rise, and led me to the entrance. In deep respect, I bowed my face down before Him.

Chapter XV

Then He answered me, and I heard His voice clearly as He said, "Do not be afraid, Enoch, righteous man and scribe of truth. Come closer and listen carefully to My words.

Go and give this message to the fallen Watchers who sent you to plead for them. It is not humans who should speak on your behalf, but you who should pray for them.

Why did you leave the high and holy heaven? Why did you take human wives and make yourselves unclean with them? You acted like earthly beings and had children with them, creating giants as your sons.

You were once pure and spiritual, living forever, yet you became corrupted by human desires. You gave in to fleshly desires, just like mortal men who are destined to die.

I gave men wives so they could have children and continue life on earth. Their needs would be met, and everything would be provided for them.

But you were different. You were created as spiritual beings, meant to live forever in heaven. That is why I did not give you wives. The heavenly ones were meant to stay in heaven, not take part in human ways.

Now, the children born from your union with human women will be known as evil spirits on earth, for that is where they belong. These spirits come from both men and fallen angels, and because of their corrupted origin, they will forever be known as wicked spirits.

The spirits of heaven will remain in heaven, but the spirits born on earth must stay on earth, as this is their rightful place.

The spirits of these giants will bring suffering, oppression, and destruction. They will fight against people, cause chaos, and bring misery to the world. They will not eat food, but they will always be hungry and thirsty. They will continue to harm others and spread pain. These spirits will rise against humanity and women because they came from them and are tied to their actions."

Chapter XVI

Since the time when the giants were destroyed, the spirits that came from their bodies have continued to bring destruction without being judged. They will keep doing this until the final day—the great day of judgment—when the world as it is now will come to an end. On that day, judgment will be carried out against the fallen Watchers and the wicked, and everything will be set right.

As for the Watchers who sent you to plead for them—those who once lived in heaven—give them this message: "You once lived in heaven, but not all its secrets were revealed to you. Instead, you only learned things that were useless and harmful. Yet, with stubborn hearts, you taught these things to human women. Because of this knowledge, both men and women have done great evil on the earth."

So, tell them this:

"You will never have peace."
Enoch's Journeys through
the Earth and Sheol

Chapter XVII

They took me to a place where the beings looked like flames of fire, but when they wanted to, they appeared as human.

They brought me to a land of deep darkness, where a massive mountain stretched all the way to the sky.

I saw where the heavenly lights were kept and the storerooms of the stars and thunder hidden deep within. There, I saw a fiery bow, arrows, a quiver, a blazing sword, and bolts of lightning flashing brightly.

They led me to flowing waters and to the fire in the west, where the sun sets each day.

I came to a river of fire, where the flames moved like rushing water and poured into the vast sea in the west.

I saw many great rivers until I reached one that led into complete darkness. Then I arrived at a place where no living creature had ever walked.

I saw the mountains covered in winter's darkness and the source where all the deep waters begin.

I saw the mouths of all the rivers on earth and the openings where the waters of the deep emerge.

Chapter XVIII

I saw the storerooms where all the winds were kept and understood how they were designed to support creation and strengthen the earth's foundations. These winds played an important role in keeping the natural world in balance.

I observed the foundation stone of the earth, the key piece that holds everything together, and I saw the four winds that support both the earth and the sky above. These winds not only kept everything stable but also acted as a force that connected heaven and earth.

I watched as the winds stretched across the sky, forming great arches and vaults. They positioned themselves between heaven and earth, acting as pillars that held up the sky and kept everything in order.

I saw the heavenly winds that guided the movement of the sun and stars, directing them to their proper places as they set each day. These winds controlled the motion of the celestial bodies, keeping the universe in its rhythm.

I also saw the winds of the earth carrying clouds across the sky. Along these winds, angels traveled, fulfilling their duties. At the farthest edge of the earth, I reached the vast expanse of the heavens. As I continued further, I arrived at a place that burned with fire both day and night. Here, seven towering mountains stood, their stones shining with an incredible beauty. Three of the mountains faced east, and three faced south.

The mountains to the east were made of rare and precious materials—one of vibrant, colorful stone, another of pure pearl, and the third of deep blue jacinth. The mountains to the south were made of glowing red stone.

The mountain in the center was the most incredible of them all. It rose so high that it reached the heavens. It looked like the very throne of God, made of pure white alabaster, and its peak sparkled with sapphire, as if crowned with divine glory.

Beyond these mountains, I saw a massive fire that burned with great intensity. Further ahead, I reached the very edge of the earth, where the sky itself came to an end, marking the boundary between the known world and the unknown.

There, I came upon a deep abyss, filled with enormous columns of heavenly fire. These flames rose and fell, reaching heights and depths beyond understanding. The abyss stretched endlessly, filled with a brilliant, consuming fire.

Beyond the abyss, I found a place unlike anything I had ever seen. There was no sky above, no solid ground below. No water, no life, not even birds flying overhead. It was an empty, terrifying wasteland, completely lifeless.

In this desolate place, I saw seven stars burning like massive mountains of fire. When I asked about them, the angel who was guiding me explained their purpose.

He said, "This is the boundary between heaven and earth. It has become a prison for the stars and the hosts of heaven. The stars that are trapped here are those that disobeyed the command of the Lord. When they were first created, they refused to rise at their appointed times and failed to fulfill their duties.

Because of their rebellion, the Lord became angry and bound them here. They will remain imprisoned in this place until the time when their punishment is complete—a period that will last for ten thousand years."

Chapter XIX

Uriel said to me, "This is the place where the angels who took human wives will remain. Their spirits take on different forms and are spreading corruption among people. They are leading humanity astray, making them worship demons as if they were gods. They will stay here until the great day of judgment, when they will be judged and destroyed.

The women who were with the angels will also be changed, becoming sirens."

And I, Enoch, was the only one who saw this vision, witnessing the fate of all things. No one else will see what I have seen.

Chapter XX

Here are the names of the holy angels who watch over everything:

- Uriel is a holy angel who is in charge of the world and the place of punishment.
- Raphael watches over the spirits of humans.
- Raguel is responsible for bringing justice to the heavenly lights.
- Michael is appointed over the best of humanity and has power over chaos.

- Saraqâêl watches over the spirits that have sinned.
- Gabriel is responsible for Paradise, the serpents, and the Cherubim.
- Remiel has been chosen by God to watch over those who will rise again.

Chapter XXI

I came to a place where everything was in complete chaos. It was unlike anything I had ever seen before—disorder and confusion filled the space.

There was no sky above me, no solid ground below, just a dark and unstable void. It felt as if the whole place was in constant turmoil, without any sense of balance or structure.

In this place, I saw seven stars that had fallen from heaven. They were massive, like towering mountains, and each one was surrounded by intense flames, burning brightly. The fire engulfed them, making the sight both fascinating and terrifying.

I asked, "Why have these stars been bound here? What did they do to deserve this punishment?"

Uriel, the holy angel who was with me and in charge of them, answered, "Enoch, why do you ask? Why do you want to understand this so deeply? These stars were among the heavenly beings who disobeyed the Lord's command. Because they broke His law, they were cast into this place, where they will remain for ten thousand years until their punishment is complete."

After that, I was taken to another place, even more terrifying than the first. The sight before me was beyond words, filling me with overwhelming fear.

A massive fire burned endlessly, its flames alive and consuming everything around them. The fire stretched deep into the abyss, with enormous columns of flame shooting downward. The size and power of the fire were beyond understanding—it seemed to go on forever, with no end in sight.

I cried out, "This place is horrifying! Just looking at it is unbearable!"

Uriel, the holy angel beside me, turned and said, "Enoch, why are you so afraid? Why does this place trouble you so much?"

I answered, "I am overwhelmed by the sheer terror of this place and the suffering that happens here."

Uriel then explained, "This is the prison of the fallen angels. They will remain here, bound and imprisoned, for all eternity."

Chapter XXII

I was taken to another place, where I saw a massive mountain in the west. It was made of solid rock, towering over everything, its surface hard and unbreakable. The mountain stood like a great monument, both impressive and intimidating.

Inside this mountain, I saw four large hollow spaces. Each one was deep, wide, and incredibly smooth, as if shaped with perfect precision. They stretched far into the darkness. Three of them were completely dark, while the fourth shone brightly, with a spring of water flowing at its center. Looking at them, I said, "These hollow spaces are so smooth and deep! They seem mysterious and almost endless."

Raphael, one of the holy angels with me, explained their purpose. He said, "These hollow spaces were made to hold the spirits of the dead. All human souls come here after death. They remain here until the time set for their judgment, waiting for the great day when justice will be carried out."

I saw the spirits of the dead gathered there, their voices rising in sorrow, pleading to heaven. I turned to Raphael and asked, "Whose spirit is crying out so desperately?"

He answered, "This is the spirit of Abel, who was killed by his brother Cain. Abel's voice calls for justice against Cain. His cry will continue until Cain's descendants are completely removed from the earth and no longer exist among mankind."

Then I asked about the different hollow spaces, wondering why they were separated. "Why are these places divided? What is the reason for keeping them apart?"

Raphael explained, "These spaces are divided to separate the spirits of the dead based on their deeds in life. One space is for the righteous, where the bright spring of water flows, bringing them peace and light. Another is for sinners—those who were buried after death but never faced judgment while alive. Their spirits suffer in great pain, waiting for the day of judgment. When that time comes, they will face punishment and eternal torment for their actions. They will remain bound here forever."

He continued, "There is also a space for the spirits of those who died violently during times of great sin. Their cries reveal the details of their destruction. Another space is for those who lived in complete rebellion, breaking all laws and rejecting righteousness. These spirits stay together, sharing in their guilt. But on the day of judgment, their spirits will not be completely destroyed, nor will they ever rise again from this place."

Hearing and seeing all of this, I was overwhelmed by the deep mysteries revealed to me. In awe and reverence, I praised the Lord of Glory, saying, "Blessed are You, Lord of righteousness, who rules over everything and reigns forever."

Chapter XXIII

From there, I traveled to the farthest part of the west, reaching the very edge of the earth. This place was unlike anything I had ever seen, filled with a strange and endless phenomenon.

In front of me, a massive fire burned fiercely. It never stayed still but moved constantly, day and night, without ever stopping. It followed a set path, never slowing down, its flames burning with steady intensity. The way it moved made it seem like it had a purpose, and the sight of it was both fascinating and unsettling.

Curious, I asked, "What is this fire that never stops? What is its purpose, and why does it keep moving without rest?"

Raguel, one of the holy angels with me, answered, "This is the fire of the west. It is the force that guides and drives the heavenly lights, making sure they follow their paths and fulfill their duties in the sky."

As I listened to his words, I was amazed by the perfect order and precision that controlled even this unstoppable fire. It was not chaotic but part of a greater system that kept the heavens and earth in balance. Seeing this filled me with awe and a deeper understanding of how creation was carefully designed.

Chapter XXIV

From there, I traveled to another place on earth, where I saw a range of mountains covered in fire. The flames burned endlessly, day and night, rising high into the sky and lighting up everything around them.

Beyond these fiery mountains, I saw something even more incredible—seven magnificent mountains, each one unique and different from the others. They were made of rare and beautiful stones, their appearance grand and breathtaking. The stones shined brightly, their surfaces smooth and flawless.

Three of the mountains stood in the east, stacked one on top of another, forming a towering structure. Another three stood to the south, also layered in the same way. Deep and rugged valleys lay between them, separating each mountain completely. None of these valleys connected, making the landscape wild and untouched.

In the center of them all stood the seventh mountain, the tallest and most majestic of them. Its peak looked like a throne, strong and powerful, surrounded by fragrant trees that filled the air with a sweet aroma.

Among these trees, I saw one unlike anything I had ever encountered. Its scent was stronger and sweeter than any fragrance I had ever known. Its leaves, blossoms, and wood never faded or withered—they remained perfect forever. The fruit of this tree was breathtaking, more beautiful than any other, similar to dates from a palm tree but even more magnificent.

I marveled at the sight and said, "This tree is so beautiful! Its fragrance is amazing, its leaves are so pleasing, and its blossoms are wonderful to look at."

Then Michael, one of the honored and holy angels who was with me and served as their leader, answered me.

Chapter XXV

He said to me, "Enoch, why do you ask about the scent of this tree? Why are you so eager to understand its meaning?"

I replied, "I want to understand everything, but I am especially curious about this tree and its importance."

Then he explained, "The great mountain you saw, with its peak shaped like a throne, is indeed the throne of God. This is where the Holy Great One, the Lord of Glory, the Eternal King, will sit when He comes down to visit the earth in His power and goodness.

As for this fragrant tree, no human is allowed to touch it until the great day of judgment. On that day, when He brings justice to all and fulfills His eternal plan, the tree will be given to the righteous and the holy. They will eat its fruit, and the tree itself will be moved to the sacred place—the temple of the Lord, the Eternal King.

At that time, the righteous will be filled with joy and happiness. They will enter the holy place, and the scent of this tree will fill them with life. They will live long and fulfilling lives on earth, just as their ancestors did. In their time, there will be no sorrow, disease, pain, or disaster. They will live in peace and harmony."

Hearing these words, I praised the God of Glory, the Eternal King, who has prepared such wonderful things for the righteous. I thanked Him for creating and promising these blessings to those who are holy and chosen.

Chapter XXVI

I traveled from there to the center of the earth, where I saw a land overflowing with blessings. The area was covered with lush trees, their branches full of life and blooming with beauty. It felt as if they carried the essence of something ancient, once divided but now thriving again.

In this land, I saw a majestic holy mountain rising high above everything. Beneath it, on the eastern side, a peaceful stream of water flowed smoothly toward the south, its path steady and undisturbed.

Looking further east, I saw another mountain, even taller than the first. Between these two mountains was a deep, narrow ravine, carved into the land like a natural divide. Within this ravine, another stream flowed beneath the towering mountain, its waters hidden yet always moving.

To the west of the first mountain, I noticed a smaller mountain, not as tall or imposing as the others. Between this smaller mountain and the first one, there was another ravine. Unlike the others, this ravine was dry and lifeless, with no flowing water. At the far edges of all three mountains, another deep and dry ravine stretched out, marking the end of the landscape.

The ravines I saw were narrow and incredibly deep, cutting through solid rock. Their walls were bare, with no trees or plants growing on them. The land was rough and unyielding, its vast emptiness creating a sharp contrast to the lush greenery I had seen earlier.

I stood in awe, amazed by the jagged cliffs and towering rock formations of the ravines. The difference between the lifeless, rocky terrain and the beautiful, flourishing land nearby filled me with wonder. I couldn't help but marvel at the incredible sights before me.

Chapter XXVII

Then I asked, "What is the purpose of this blessed land, so full of life and covered with flourishing trees? And why does this cursed valley lie between them?"

Uriel, one of the holy angels with me, answered, "This cursed valley is meant for those who are forever condemned. It is where all who have spoken disrespectfully and falsely against the Lord will be gathered. Those who have insulted Him, spoken against His glory, or defied His name will be brought here for judgment.

This is where they will face justice. When the final days come and the righteous are judged, these people will be punished in front of them. This valley will be their dwelling place, a lasting reminder of their rebellion and the consequences of their actions.

At the same time, the faithful and righteous will bless the Lord of Glory, the Eternal King, in this very place. They will praise Him with gratitude, giving thanks for His justice. They will honor Him for showing mercy to the righteous and giving them their rightful place in His plan.

When judgment is carried out on the wicked, the righteous will glorify the Lord even more. They will celebrate the kindness He has shown them by granting them peace and salvation. They will see how fair He is in judging the wicked and recognize His perfect justice."

Overwhelmed by everything I had seen and heard, I blessed the Lord of Glory. I proclaimed His greatness, praising His name with deep gratitude. I lifted my voice to honor the Eternal King, who rules with righteousness and mercy forever.

Chapter XXVIII

From there, I traveled east and entered a vast desert surrounded by mountains. The land was quiet and empty, yet different kinds of trees and plants grew in its stillness.

Water poured down from above, rushing like a powerful river. The strong current flowed toward the northwest, moving with great force. As it traveled, the water created clouds and mist, spreading moisture across the land.

Chapter XXIX

From there, I traveled to another area in the desert, heading toward the eastern side of the mountain range.

There, I saw trees that released a rich and pleasant fragrance, filling the air with the sweet scents of frankincense and myrrh. The trees looked similar to almond trees, with their branches and shapes resembling them closely.

Chapter XXX

Beyond these places, I traveled farther east and arrived at a valley filled with water.

In this valley, I saw a tree that looked and smelled like other fragrant trees, similar to the mastic tree.

Along the sides of the valley, I noticed cinnamon trees growing, releasing their sweet scent into the air. From there, I continued my journey even farther east.

Chapter XXXI

I saw more mountains, and among them were groves of trees. These trees produced a sweet, fragrant sap known as sarara and galbanum.

Beyond these mountains, I reached another mountain at the far eastern edge of the earth. This mountain was covered with aloe trees, and their branches were filled with a substance called stacte. The trees had a shape similar to almond trees.

When the sap from these trees was burned, it released a scent that was sweeter and more pleasant than any other fragrance.

Chapter XXXII

After taking in these wonderful scents, I looked to the north, beyond the mountains, and saw seven peaks covered with the finest nard, fragrant trees, cinnamon, and pepper.

To the northeast, I saw another group of seven mountains, also filled with the best nard, mastic, cinnamon, and pepper.

From there, I traveled across the peaks of all these mountains, continuing far toward the easternmost parts of the earth. I passed over the Erythraean Sea and went even farther, crossing into the region of the angel Zotîêl.

Eventually, I arrived at the Garden of Righteousness. Beyond all the trees I had seen before, I found even more—huge, breathtaking trees that were full of beauty and fragrance. Among them stood a very special tree—the tree of wisdom, whose fruit gives great knowledge to those who eat it.

This tree stood tall, as high as a fir, with leaves that looked like those of a carob tree. Its fruit grew in clusters, like grapes on a vine, and was incredibly beautiful. Its fragrance was so strong that it spread far across the land.

Amazed, I said, "This tree is so beautiful! Its appearance is so inviting!"

Then Raphael, the holy angel who was with me, answered, "This is the tree of wisdom. It is the same tree that your ancient father and mother ate from long ago. When they ate its fruit, they gained wisdom, their eyes were opened, and they realized they were naked. Because of this, they were sent out of the garden."

Chapter XXXIII

From there, I traveled to the farthest ends of the earth, where I saw great and powerful creatures. Each one was unique, with different shapes and appearances. I also saw many birds, each with its own beauty, size, and voice. No two were the same, making the scene even more amazing.

To the east of these creatures, I reached the very edge of the earth, where the heavens touch it. There, I saw openings in the sky, where the heavens seemed to connect to the land.

I watched as the stars of the sky passed through these openings. I carefully counted each one and recorded their paths. I noted where each star came from, its name, the route it followed, its position in the sky, and the times and months when it appeared.

Uriel, the holy angel who was with me, explained everything in great detail. He made sure I understood and wrote it all down. He also recorded for me the names of the stars, the rules they follow, and the groups they belong to, so that none of this knowledge would be forgotten.

Chapter XXXIV

From there, I traveled north, reaching the very edge of the earth. There, I saw an incredible and awe-inspiring structure at the boundary of the world.

I noticed three openings in the sky facing north. Through each of these openings, the winds of the north blew down to the earth. When they passed through, they brought cold air, hail, frost, snow, dew, and rain.

One of these openings released a gentle wind that brought blessings to the earth. However, the other two released powerful, violent winds. These strong winds caused trouble, bringing destruction and hardship wherever they went.

Chapter XXXV

From there, I traveled west, reaching the farthest edge of the earth. There, I saw three openings in the sky, just like the ones I had seen in the east. The number of openings and the way they released their winds were exactly the same as the ones I had observed before.

Chapter XXXVI

From there, I traveled south to the farthest edge of the earth. There, I saw three open portals in the sky, where dew, rain, and wind flowed out, bringing life and movement to the land.

After that, I traveled east until I reached the edge of the heavens. There, I saw three more openings in the sky, just like the ones before, but above them were smaller openings.

Through these smaller openings, the stars moved along their set paths. They traveled from east to west, following the course that had been assigned to them.

Each time I saw these amazing things, I praised the Lord of Glory. I continued to honor Him, recognizing His incredible works. These wonders were not just shown to me, but also to the angels, spirits, and all people, so that everyone could see His power and give Him the honor He deserves.

His creation reveals the greatness of His power and the beauty of His design. I blessed the work of His hands and gave Him praise forever for all that He has made and revealed to His creation.

The Parables

Chapter XXXVII

The second vision that Enoch, the son of Jared, the son of Mahalalel, the son of Cainan, the son of Enos, the son of Seth, and the son of Adam, received was a vision of wisdom.

This is the beginning of the words of wisdom that I spoke, sharing them with those who live on the earth. I said, "Listen, people of the past, and pay attention, those who will come after, to the words of the Holy One that I will speak before the Lord of Spirits."

It might have seemed best to share these words only with those who lived long ago, but wisdom is not meant to be kept from future generations.

Until now, this wisdom had never been revealed by the Lord of Spirits. But according to His will, I have been given this understanding. It is by His choice that I have received the gift of eternal life.

Three parables were shown to me, and I raised my voice to share them with those who live on the earth.

The First Parable

Chapter XXXVIII

When the time comes for the gathering of the righteous and the judgment of sinners, those who have done evil will be removed from the earth. They will be completely separated from the righteous and will no longer have a place among the living.

When the Righteous One is revealed before the eyes of those who have remained faithful—those whose good deeds are recognized by the Lord of Spirits—His light will shine upon them. But in that moment, where will the sinners go? Where will those who rejected the Lord of Spirits find rest? It would have been better for them if they had never been born.

When the hidden truths of the righteous are made known, and the sinners are judged, those who rejected God will be cast far away. They will be completely removed, with no place left for their corruption among the holy and chosen ones.

From that moment on, those who once ruled with pride and power will lose their high status. They will no longer be able to look upon the faces of the holy, because the Lord of Spirits will shine His glorious light upon the righteous and chosen ones. His brilliance will be too great for them to bear.

Then, the kings of the earth and the mighty ones will be destroyed, and they will be given over to the righteous and holy. Their power will disappear, and they will fall into the hands of those who remained faithful to the Lord.

After that, no one will ask the Lord of Spirits for mercy, because their time of life will be over. Their chance to repent will be gone, and they will receive the full judgment they deserve.

Chapter XXXIX

In those days, the chosen and holy ones will come down from the heavens, and their descendants will live among the people on earth.

During that time, Enoch received books filled with messages of justice, anger, and judgment, along with records of trouble and exile. The Lord of Spirits declared that those who were judged would not receive mercy.

In those days, a powerful wind lifted me from the earth and carried me to the farthest parts of the heavens. There, I had another vision—one that revealed the homes of the holy and the resting places of the righteous.

I saw their dwellings alongside the righteous angels, where they rested among the holy ones. They were offering prayers and interceding on behalf of humanity. Righteousness flowed before them like a river, and mercy covered the earth like morning dew. This had been their way from the beginning and would continue forever.

In that place, I saw the Elect One, the one chosen for righteousness and faith. He lived under the protection of the Lord of Spirits. In His time, righteousness would flourish, and the number of the chosen ones standing before Him would be endless, lasting forever.

All the righteous and chosen ones will shine like flames of fire. Their mouths will be filled with blessings, and they will speak the name of the Lord of Spirits with praise. Righteousness will always stand before Him, unshaken, and goodness will last forever in His presence.

At that moment, I wished to stay there. My spirit longed for the peace and beauty of that place, for it had already been set apart for me by the Lord of Spirits. It had been prepared long ago, and I desired to remain there forever.

During those days, I lifted my voice in praise, blessing the name of the Lord of Spirits with words of gratitude. I honored Him for the glory and blessings He had planned for me, according to His will and kindness.

For a long time, I gazed at that place, continuing to bless and praise Him, saying, "Blessed is He, and may His name be praised forever and ever. Before Him, there is no beginning or end, for He knows everything, even before the world was created. He sees all that will happen through every generation."

Those who never sleep stand before His glory, constantly blessing and praising Him. They continuously declare, "Holy, holy, holy is the Lord of Spirits. He fills the earth with His presence."

I saw these beings with my own eyes—those who never rest, who stand before Him, offering endless praise. They said, "Blessed are You, and blessed is the name of the Lord forever and ever."

At that moment, my face changed, for I could no longer handle the overwhelming brightness of His glory.

Chapter XL

After that, I saw a crowd so huge that it was impossible to count—thousands upon thousands, and ten thousand times ten thousand—standing before the

Lord of Spirits. The gathering was beyond measure, like an endless sea of beings.

Around the Lord of Spirits, I saw four powerful beings, different from the ones who never sleep. The angel who was with me told me their names and revealed hidden truths about them.

I listened as these four beings spoke, offering praises before the Lord of Glory:

The first voice gave blessings to the Lord of Spirits, praising Him forever.

The second voice blessed the Elect One and the chosen people who put their trust in the Lord of Spirits.

The third voice prayed on behalf of the people on earth, bringing their requests before the Lord of Spirits.

The fourth voice stood against the Satans, preventing them from approaching the Lord of Spirits to accuse the people of the earth.

Curious, I turned to the angel of peace, who was with me and revealed hidden things, and I asked, "Who are these four beings I have seen, whose voices I have heard and recorded?"

He answered, "The first is Michael, known for his mercy and patience. The second is Raphael, who is responsible for healing, caring for the sicknesses and wounds of people. The third is Gabriel, who has power over all authorities and forces. The fourth is Phanuel, who leads those who repent and brings hope to those chosen for eternal life. These are the four angels of the Lord of Spirits, and the voices you heard belong to them."

Chapter XLI

After that, I was shown all the secrets of the heavens—how the kingdom is divided and how human actions are judged with perfect fairness.

I saw where the chosen ones live and the homes of the holy. I also saw sinners being removed, those who had rejected the name of the Lord of Spirits. They were taken away and could not stay because of the punishment sent by Him.

In that place, I was also shown the secrets of lightning and thunder—how they are formed and where they come from. I learned about the winds, how they are separated and sent across the earth, and the mysteries of the clouds and dew—where they originate and how they bring moisture to dry land.

I saw the places where the winds are stored, as well as the chambers of hail, mist, and clouds. The clouds remain above the earth, just as they have since the beginning of time.

I was also shown the chambers of the sun and the moon, the places where their journeys begin and where they return. I watched their bright paths, noticing how the sun is greater than the moon. Their movements are steady and unchanging, never straying from their paths. They remain in harmony, following the promise they made.

The sun begins its journey first, traveling its path exactly as commanded by the Lord of Spirits. His name is great and powerful forever.

Then I saw both the seen and hidden paths of the moon. She follows her course day and night, always positioned opposite to the sun, standing before the Lord of Spirits. The sun and the moon constantly give thanks and praise, never resting, for their rest comes from their worship.

The sun sometimes changes its course, bringing either blessings or hardships. The moon, however, brings light to the righteous and darkness to sinners, all according to the will of the Lord. He is the one who separated light from darkness, dividing the spirits of people—strengthening the righteous through His name and justice.

No angel or power can interfere with these paths. The Lord is the one who appoints a judge over everything, and He alone decides what is right in His presence.

Chapter XLII

Wisdom searched for a place to live, but she could not find one. So, a home was made for her in the heavens.

She then went down to live among people, but there was no place for her to stay. Since she could not remain among them, she returned to her rightful place and sat among the angels.

At the same time, unrighteousness left its dwelling and found those who had not been looking for it. It settled among them, like rain falling on a dry desert or dew resting on thirsty ground.

Chapter XLIII

I saw flashes of lightning and the stars in the sky. I watched as He called each one by name, and they listened and followed His command.

I saw how they were measured with perfect fairness based on the brightness of their light. I observed the space they filled, the times they appeared, and how their movements created flashes of lightning. I also saw how their paths were connected to the number of angels and how they remained faithful to their courses and to each other.

Then I turned to the angel who was with me, the one who revealed hidden things, and I asked, "What do these mean?"

He answered, "The Lord of Spirits has shown you their deeper meaning. These represent the names of the holy ones who live on the earth and believe in the name of the Lord of Spirits forever."

Chapter XLIV

I also noticed something unusual about the lightning. I saw some stars rise up and change into flashes of lightning. Once they transformed, they could never return to the way they were before.

The Second Parable

The destiny of those who reject the truth and the hope of a new heaven and a new earth.

Chapter XLV

This is the second message about those who reject the home of the holy ones and the Lord of Spirits.

They will not rise to heaven, nor will they stay on the earth. This will be the fate of those who denied the name of the Lord of Spirits. They are being kept for a day of suffering and hardship.

On that day, My Chosen One will sit on the throne of glory and judge their actions. There will be countless places of rest for the righteous. Their spirits will be strengthened when they see My Chosen Ones and those who have called upon My glorious name.

At that time, I will make My Chosen One live among them. I will transform the heavens into an everlasting source of blessing and light.

I will also renew the earth, making it a land of blessing. My chosen people will live there, but sinners and wrongdoers will not be allowed to enter.

I have prepared this peaceful place as a home for the righteous, where they will live before Me. But for the sinners, judgment is coming. I will remove them from the earth forever.

Chapter XLVI

There, I saw One who was very old, with hair as white as wool. Beside Him stood another being who looked like a man. His face was kind and full of grace, resembling one of the holy angels.

I turned to the angel who was with me, the one revealing all the hidden things, and asked about this Son of Man—who He was, where He came from, and why He was standing with the Ancient One.

The angel answered, "This is the Son of Man, the righteous one, in whom all righteousness dwells. He reveals hidden treasures because the Lord of Spirits has chosen Him. He has been given honor before the Lord of Spirits, and His righteousness will last forever.

"This Son of Man you see will bring down kings and powerful rulers from their thrones. He will take away the strength of the mighty and break the power of sinners. He will humble the rulers of the world and remove their kingdoms because they failed to honor and praise Him or recognize the One who gave them their authority.

"He will disgrace the proud and the powerful, casting them into complete darkness. That darkness will be their home forever. They will lie in the dust like worms, with no hope of ever rising again. This will happen because they refused to praise the name of the Lord of Spirits.

"These are the ones who tried to control the stars of heaven and lifted their hands in rebellion against the Most High. They ruled the earth in corruption, living unrighteously. Their power came from their wealth, and they put their trust in idols they made with their own hands. They denied the name of the Lord of Spirits.

"They also attacked the homes of His people and persecuted the faithful who trust in the name of the Lord of Spirits."

Chapter XLVII

In those days, the prayers of the righteous and the cries of those whose blood was spilled on the earth will rise up before the Lord of Spirits.

At that time, the holy ones in heaven will come together as one. They will pray, plead, and give thanks, blessing the name of the Lord of Spirits. They will ask that the blood of the righteous be remembered, that their prayers are not ignored, and that justice is done for them so they will no longer suffer forever.

During that time, I saw the Ancient One seated on His glorious throne. Before Him, the books of the living were opened, and all the heavenly beings and His advisors stood in His presence.

The hearts of the holy ones were filled with joy because the number of the righteous was complete. Their prayers had been heard, and the blood of the righteous had been acknowledged and avenged before the Lord of Spirits.

Chapter XLVIII

In that place, I saw a fountain of righteousness that never dried up. Around it were many fountains of wisdom, and everyone who was thirsty drank from them, filling themselves with wisdom. They lived among the righteous, the holy, and the chosen ones.

At that moment, the Son of Man was named before the Lord of Spirits, and His name was declared in the presence of the Ancient One. Even before the sun, the stars, and the heavenly signs were created, His name was already known to the Lord of Spirits.

He will be a guide for the righteous, keeping them from stumbling. He will be a light for the nations and a source of hope for those with troubled hearts.

Everyone on earth will bow before Him, worshiping and singing songs of praise to the Lord of Spirits.

For this reason, He was chosen and set apart long before the world was created, and He will remain forever. The wisdom of the Lord of Spirits revealed Him to the holy and righteous. He has protected the chosen ones because they rejected the wickedness of this world and refused to follow its evil ways. Through His name, they are saved, and by His will, their lives are kept safe.

During that time, the kings and rulers of the earth—those who held power—will bow their heads in shame because of the sinful things they have done. When their time of suffering comes, they will be helpless and unable to save themselves.

The Lord will hand them over to His chosen ones. They will burn like straw in the fire before the holy ones. Like lead sinking in water, they will disappear before the righteous, leaving nothing behind.

On that day of suffering, there will be peace on the earth. The wicked will fall and never rise again. No one will help them or lift them up, because they denied the Lord of Spirits and His Anointed One.

May the name of the Lord of Spirits be blessed forever.

Chapter XLIX

Wisdom flows like water, and His glory never fades—it lasts forever. He holds the power over all the secrets of righteousness, and evil will disappear like a passing shadow, never to return. This is because the Chosen One stands before the Lord of Spirits. His glory will never end, and His strength will last for all generations.

Within Him is the spirit of wisdom and understanding. He has the spirit of insight, strength, and the spirit of those who have lived in righteousness. He will judge all hidden things, and no one will be able to lie in His presence.

He is the Chosen One, selected by the Lord of Spirits, exactly as He willed.

Chapter L

In those days, the holy and chosen ones will experience a great transformation. The light of the days will shine on them, and they will be clothed in glory and honor. This will happen when the time of trouble comes, and the sins of the wicked are fully exposed and held against them. On that day, the righteous will be victorious in the name of the Lord of Spirits. He will allow others to see this, giving them a chance to turn away from their wrongdoings, repent, and leave behind their evil ways.

Even though they will not receive honor through the name of the Lord of Spirits, they will still have the opportunity to be saved by it. The Lord of Spirits will show them mercy because His compassion has no limits. However, He is also a just judge, and no evil will stand in His presence. Those who refuse to repent will be destroyed when judgment comes.

From that moment on, there will be no mercy for those who refuse to turn back, says the Lord of Spirits.

Chapter LI

In those days, the earth will return what was buried in it, Sheol will give back those it has received, and hell will release what it owes. During this time, the Chosen One, selected by the Lord of Spirits, will rise. He will separate the righteous and holy from everyone else, because the time for their salvation has arrived.

The Chosen One will sit on the throne prepared for him, and from his mouth will come the wisdom and guidance that have been hidden through the ages. The Lord of Spirits has given him these treasures and has honored him above all others.

On that day, the mountains will leap with joy like rams, and the hills will dance like young lambs full of milk. The faces of all the angels in heaven will shine with happiness.

The earth will celebrate with great joy, and the righteous will live upon it. The chosen ones will walk freely across the land, rejoicing in the blessings of the Lord.

Chapter LII

After those days, in the place where I had seen visions of hidden things—when a whirlwind had carried me toward the west—I saw more secrets of heaven that were yet to come. I saw a mountain of iron, a mountain of copper, a mountain of silver, a mountain of gold, a mountain of soft metal, and a mountain of lead.

I turned to the angel who was with me and asked, "What do these things mean?" He answered, "All of these mountains you see will serve the power of His Anointed One, making him strong and mighty on the earth."

Then the angel of peace said to me, "Be patient, and soon all the mysteries of the Lord of Spirits will be revealed to you. These mountains of iron, copper, silver, gold, soft metal, and lead will all melt away before the Chosen One, just like wax melts in fire or water flows down from above. They will lose their strength and crumble at his feet."

"In those days, no one will be saved by their wealth of gold or silver. No one will find a way to escape judgment. Iron will no longer be used for war, and armor will no longer be worn. Bronze will become worthless, and tin will lose its value. Lead will no longer be needed.

All these materials will be rejected and removed from the earth when the Chosen One appears before the Lord of Spirits."

Chapter LIII

After those days, in the place where I had seen visions of hidden things—when a whirlwind carried me toward the west—I saw more secrets of heaven that were yet to come. I saw a mountain of iron, a mountain of copper, a mountain of silver, a mountain of gold, a mountain of soft metal, and a mountain of lead.

I turned to the angel who was with me and asked, "What do these things mean?"

He answered, "All of these mountains you see will serve the power of His Anointed One, making him strong and mighty on the earth."

Then the angel of peace said to me, "Be patient, and soon all the mysteries of the Lord of Spirits will be revealed to you. These mountains of iron, copper, silver, gold, soft metal, and lead will all melt away before the

Chosen One, just like wax melts in fire or water flows down from above. They will lose their strength and crumble at his feet."

"In those days, no one will be saved by their gold or silver. No one will be able to escape. Iron will no longer be used for war, and armor will no longer be worn. Bronze will become worthless, tin will lose its value, and lead will no longer be needed.

All these materials will be thrown away and destroyed from the earth when the Chosen One appears before the Lord of Spirits."

Chapter LIV

After that, the Ancient One looked back and said, "It was pointless that I destroyed all who lived on the earth." Then He swore by His great name, saying,

"Never again will I do this to everyone on earth. I will place a sign in the sky—a lasting promise between Me and them forever, as long as the heavens remain above the earth. This will be done by My command."

"But when the time comes for Me to take hold of them through the hands of the angels—on the day of trouble and suffering—I will let My judgment and anger fall upon them," says the Lord of Spirits.

To the mighty rulers of the earth, the day will come when you will see My Chosen One seated on the throne of glory. He will judge Azâzêl, his followers, and all those who stand with him, carrying out justice in the name of the Lord of Spirits. His power and righteousness will be made clear before all creation, and you will witness it.

Chapter LV

I saw the armies of angels sent for punishment, moving with purpose. They carried whips, iron chains, and bronze shackles in their hands. Curious and concerned, I turned to the angel of peace who was with me and asked, "Where are these angels going with their whips and chains?"

He answered, "They are going to those who were once chosen and loved, but have turned away. They will be thrown into the deep valley as punishment for their rebellion. Their betrayal has led them here, and the valley will be filled with those who once followed them. This will be the end of their time, and they will no longer be counted among the living."

In those days, the angels will return, carrying out their mission. They will descend upon the Parthians and Medes in the east, stirring up their kings and rulers.

These kings will be filled with unrest and forced from their thrones. Like lions escaping from their dens or wolves attacking unguarded flocks, they will charge forward, spreading destruction and chaos.

Their armies will invade the land of the chosen ones, crushing everything in their path. The land will be left trampled and ruined, like a field after harvest or a road flattened for their advance. But their attack will not go as planned. The city of the righteous will stand in their way, stopping their progress. Confusion will take over, and they will turn against each other. Brothers will no longer recognize each other, and even sons will be like strangers to their own parents. The battle will be so violent that countless bodies will cover the ground, a grim sign of their own destruction.

In those days, Sheol will open its mouth wide and swallow these sinners whole. Their punishment will be complete, and their destruction final. The abyss will consume them in the presence of the chosen ones, bringing their rebellion to an irrevocable end.

This will fulfill the judgment of the Lord of Spirits, and the righteous will witness the fate of those who refused to repent.

Chapter LVI

After this, I saw another vision. I watched as a huge

number of wagons moved quickly across the sky. Riding on them were men carried by the winds, coming from the east, west, and south. Their arrival was marked by a loud roaring sound that filled the air. The rumbling of their wheels was powerful and impossible to ignore.

As their deafening approach echoed through the sky, the holy ones in heaven noticed the disturbance. Their eyes turned toward the source, and they recognized the importance of the moment. The pillars of the earth, which had remained firm since creation, shook and shifted as if in awe of what was happening. The vibrations spread far and wide, and the sound traveled from one end of the heavens to the other, reaching everything in just one day.

At that moment, everyone who saw it—both in the heavens and on the earth—fell down in reverence. They bowed low in worship to the Lord of Spirits, acknowledging His supreme power and authority. The sight was overwhelming, a reminder that even the most powerful beings recognize the greatness of the Holy One.

And with that, the second vision came to an end, leaving a lasting impression of the Lord's greatness and the fulfillment of His divine plan. The heavens and the earth stood as witnesses, testifying to His eternal glory and perfect judgment.

The Third Parable

Chapter LVII

Then I began to share the third parable, which was about the righteous and the chosen ones.

Blessed are you, the righteous and chosen ones, for your future will be filled with glory. The righteous will live in the light of the sun, while the chosen ones will shine in the light of eternal life. Their days will never end, and the lives of the holy will last forever.

They will seek the light, and through it, they will find righteousness with the Lord of Spirits. Peace will be given to the righteous, granted to them in the name of the Eternal Lord.

Afterward, the holy ones in heaven will be told to seek the secrets of righteousness, which are the inheritance of faith. These truths will shine as brightly on earth as the sun, for the time of darkness will be over.

A never-ending light will shine upon them, and their days will have no limit. Darkness will be completely destroyed, and light will stand forever before the Lord of Spirits. The brightness of righteousness will never fade, remaining strong in the presence of the Eternal Lord of Spirits.

Chapter LVIII

In those days, my eyes were opened, and I saw the mysteries of lightning and the lights and how they carry out their purpose. They flash across the sky, sometimes bringing blessings and other times bringing judgment, depending on the will of the Lord of Spirits.

I also learned the secrets of thunder and understood how its sound echoes through the heavens. When it roars, its deep rumble reaches the earth. I was shown how judgments are carried out—sometimes to bring goodness and blessings, and other times to bring punishment—all according to the command of the Lord of Spirits.

After this, all the mysteries of the lights and lightning were revealed to me. I saw how they shine and move, bringing blessings and fulfillment to the earth.

Book of Noaha Fragment

Chapter LIX

In the 500th year of my life, on the 14th day of the 7th month, I saw a vision. In this vision, a great earthquake shook the heavens, causing a disturbance among the angels of the Most High. Thousands upon thousands of them were troubled, moving in confusion.

Then, the Ancient One took His place on His glorious throne, surrounded by angels and the righteous. I was overcome with fear, and my body trembled uncontrollably. I lost all strength and collapsed to the ground, unable to bear what I was seeing. Then Michael sent another holy angel to help me. The angel lifted me up, and my spirit returned because I couldn't endure the vision on my own.

Michael spoke to me and said, "Why are you so troubled by this vision? Until now, the Lord of Spirits has shown patience and mercy to those on earth. But the time for judgment is coming. When that day arrives, the Lord will bring justice upon those who reject His ways, refuse to do what is right, and dishonor His name. For the chosen ones, it will be a day of salvation, but for sinners, it will be a time of judgment and punishment."

"The punishment of the Lord of Spirits will not be without purpose. It will come upon the wicked so that His justice is fulfilled. Even families—parents and children—will face judgment together, but in the end, His mercy and patience will remain in His final decision."

On that same day, two great monsters were separated. One, a female named Leviathan, was sent to live in the deep ocean above the fountains of the waters. The other, a male named Behemoth, was placed in a barren wilderness called Dûidâin, to the east of the land of the chosen ones—the same place where my ancestor, the seventh from Adam, was taken up by the Lord of Spirits.

I asked one of the angels to show me the power of these creatures and explain why they were separated—one in the sea and the other in the dry wilderness. The angel replied, "Son of man, you are asking about hidden things."

Then another angel, who was with me, began to reveal the mysteries of creation. He spoke of the heights of heaven, the depths of the earth, the edges of the universe, and the very foundations of existence. He showed me the chambers of the winds, explaining how they are divided, measured, and guided through different portals according to their strength.

He also explained the forces that move the moon and the stars, revealing their names and the order in which they travel.

I learned about thunder and where it rests before it sounds, as well as how lightning is released alongside it. Thunder and lightning are connected, moving together under the power of the spirit, yet they remain separate in their roles. They are perfectly in sync, never acting apart from each other.

When lightning flashes, thunder follows with a mighty roar. The spirit controls the timing between them, keeping them balanced. The sound of thunder is powerful, like grains of sand being scattered, and each strike is held back and released at the right moment. The spirit guides it across different parts of the earth, sending it exactly where it needs to go.

The spirit of the sea is strong and mighty, controlling the waters with great power. It pulls the waves back with immense force and then pushes them forward, sending them crashing against the mountains.

The spirit of frost is guided by an angel, and the spirit of hail is watched over by another kind and gentle angel. The spirit of snow moves with its own power, and within it, there is something special—when it rises, it looks like smoke, and it is called frost.

The spirit of mist is different from the others. It does not stay in the same chambers as them but moves on a separate path. Its journey is magnificent, flowing through light and darkness, summer and winter, and an angel is assigned to oversee it.

The spirit of dew comes from the farthest reaches of heaven, connected to the chambers of rain. It moves through winter and summer, interacting with the clouds of mist as they give and receive from one another.

When the spirit of rain is released from its chamber, angels open the doors and guide it. As it spreads across the land, it joins with the waters already present, bringing life and nourishment to the earth.

These waters are essential for all who live on the land. They feed the soil according to the command of the Most High, and for this reason, rainfall is carefully measured and assigned to angels who oversee it.

As I watched these wonders, I looked toward the Garden of the Righteous. The angel of peace, who was with me, explained, "These two great creatures, created by God's power, have been prepared for a purpose that has not yet been fulfilled."

Chapter LX

In those days, I saw long measuring cords given to the angels. They took these cords, spread their wings, and flew toward the north. Curious, I turned to the angel guiding me and asked, "Why did they take these cords and leave?" He answered, "They have gone to measure."

The angel with me explained further, "These angels are carrying the measurements meant for the righteous. They bring the cords of justice so that those who follow the Lord of Spirits will be strengthened and have a solid foundation forever. The chosen ones will live among the chosen, and these measures will serve as a symbol of faith, upholding righteousness."

"These measurements will also reveal the hidden things of the earth, including the fate of those who were lost in the desert, taken by wild animals, or drowned in the sea. All will be restored and made to stand again on the day of the Chosen One. No one will be completely lost before the Lord of Spirits, for He sees everything."

In heaven, all who lived above received a command that united them with one purpose, granting them a single voice and a light as bright as fire. With their first words, they blessed the Lord, praising His wisdom. Their speech was full of understanding, and their spirits were overflowing with life.

The Lord of Spirits placed the Chosen One upon the throne of glory. From this throne, He will judge the deeds of the holy ones in heaven. Their actions will be weighed, and when He lifts His face to give judgment, He will examine their hidden ways according to the righteousness of the Lord's name. Their paths will be measured by divine justice.

In that moment, all will join their voices in praise, glorifying, honoring, and blessing the Lord of Spirits.

On that day, the entire heavenly host will be gathered. This includes all the holy ones above, God's mighty army, the Cherubim, Seraphim, Ophanim, and every angel of power and authority. The Chosen One will stand among them, along with other great beings that govern the earth and the waters.

Together, they will raise their voices as one, blessing and praising the Lord of Spirits. They will glorify Him with faith, wisdom, patience, mercy, judgment, peace, and goodness, all declaring in unity:

"Blessed is He, and may the name of the Lord of Spirits be praised forever and ever."

All who never sleep in the heavens above will bless Him. Every holy being in heaven, every chosen soul in the garden of life, and every spirit of light capable of praising and glorifying Him will give Him honor. All people on earth will lift up His name, magnifying Him without limit, giving Him glory forever.

For the mercy of the Lord of Spirits is endless, and His patience never runs out. He has revealed all His works and everything He has created to the righteous and the chosen ones. Through His name, they witness the fullness of His glory and the depth of His love.

Chapter LXI

The Lord gave a command to the kings, rulers, and all who hold power on the earth, saying, "Open your eyes and look up if you can recognize the Chosen One." The Lord of Spirits placed the Chosen One on His glorious throne and filled Him with the spirit of righteousness. With just His words, He will bring judgment, and no sinner will be able to stand before Him.

On that day, the kings, leaders, and those in power will rise up and see the Chosen One sitting on His throne of glory. They will understand that righteousness is judged before Him, and no lies or deception can exist in His presence. At that moment, they will be filled with fear, just like a woman in pain during childbirth. The terror will be unbearable as they realize their fate.

They will look at each other in horror, but no one will have answers. Fear and confusion will grip them as they see the Son of Man on His throne. In their desperation, the kings and rulers will start to praise and worship Him, realizing He is the one they had ignored for so long.

From the very beginning, the Son of Man was hidden, kept by the Most High, and revealed only to the righteous. But on this day, the holy and chosen ones will thrive. All who have been faithful will stand before Him, while the kings and rulers will bow low, falling on their faces in worship. They will beg for mercy, hoping to be forgiven.

But judgment will not be stopped. The Lord of Spirits will declare justice upon them, and they will flee in shame, their faces filled with humiliation. They will be handed over to the angels for punishment because of the suffering they brought upon the righteous and the chosen ones.

The righteous will see their oppressors punished and will rejoice, for the wrath of the Lord will be carried out. His sword will be covered in their blood, and on that day, the righteous and chosen ones will be saved. They will never again have to live among sinners or the wicked.

The Lord of Spirits will live among the righteous, and they will share eternity with the Son of Man. They will eat, rest, and rise with Him forever, never to be separated again.

The righteous and chosen ones will be lifted from the earth, and their sorrow will turn to joy. The Lord of Spirits will clothe them in garments of glory, robes that will never grow old or fade.

These garments will be garments of life, shining forever before the Lord of Spirits, a sign of their righteousness and the eternal glory of their Creator.

Chapter LXII

In those days, the powerful rulers and kings who once ruled the earth will beg for mercy. They will plead with the angels of punishment, hoping for even a brief moment of relief. Desperate, they will wish for a chance to bow down before the Lord of Spirits and admit their sins.

They will praise and glorify the Lord, saying:

"Blessed is the Lord of Spirits, the King of all kings, the Ruler over the mighty, and the Lord of the rich. He is the Lord of glory and wisdom. His power is beyond understanding, hidden in all things, and lasts from generation to generation. His greatness never fades. His wisdom is deep, and His righteousness is beyond measure."

Then they will say:

"Now we finally understand that we should have honored and praised the Lord of kings, the One who rules over all. If only we had the chance to rest, to give thanks, and to declare our faith before His glory! But now, we can find no peace. We search for light, but it has left us. We are trapped in darkness forever."

They will realize their mistake and cry out:

"We never truly believed in Him. We did not honor the name of the Lord of Spirits. Instead, we trusted in our power, our wealth, and the kingdoms we built. But now, in this time of suffering, He does not save us. There is no relief. Now we must admit that our Lord is just in all His actions, that His judgments are fair, and that He treats all people with righteousness.

But it is too late. Because of our actions, we are cast out of His presence. Every one of our sins has been counted, and we must face the consequences."

They will mourn within themselves, saying:

"Our souls are weighed down by the wealth and power we chased after, but none of it can save us now. We are falling into the deep darkness of Sheol, and nothing can stop it."

Shame and regret will cover their faces as they stand before the Son of Man. But they will be cast out, no longer able to see His light. The sword of judgment will remain against them, cutting off any hope of mercy.

Then the Lord of Spirits will declare:

"This is the final judgment for the mighty, the kings, the rulers, and all those who held power on the earth. This is their fate before the Lord of Spirits."

Chapter LXIII

In that place, I saw beings that were hidden from sight, their true nature unknown. As I wondered about them, I heard the voice of an angel explaining their presence.

The angel said, "These are the angels who came down to earth and revealed secrets that were never meant to be known by humans. They misled people, teaching them things that led them into sin and turned them away from the path of righteousness."

Chapter LXIV

In those days, Noah saw that the earth was sinking and that its destruction was near. Feeling troubled, he traveled far, crying out loudly for his grandfather, Enoch. With deep sorrow in his voice, Noah called out three times, "Hear me! Hear me! Hear me!"

I answered him, asking, "What is happening to the earth? Why is it in such a terrible state, shaking as if it is about to collapse? Will I be destroyed along with it?"

Suddenly, the earth shook violently, and a voice echoed from the heavens. Overwhelmed by fear, I fell face down on the ground. At that moment, my grandfather Enoch appeared beside me and asked, "Why are you crying out to me with such sorrow?"

Then Enoch explained, "The Lord has given a command about those who live on the earth. Their destruction has been decided because they have uncovered the secrets of the angels—things that were never meant for them to know. They have learned the violent ways of the Satans, their powers, and forbidden knowledge. They have practiced sorcery, witchcraft, and the making of idols, corrupting the earth.

They have even discovered how to extract silver from the ground and how certain metals are formed deep within the earth. Lead and tin do not form in the same way as other metals; they come from a special source, and an angel oversees their creation. This knowledge was never meant for humans, yet they have misused it."

Then Enoch took my hand, helped me stand, and said, "Go now, for I have asked the Lord of Spirits about this great disaster. He told me, 'Because of their wickedness, judgment has been set and will not be delayed. Their love for forbidden knowledge and sorcery has sealed their fate, and the earth, along with its people, will be destroyed.'"

Enoch continued, "There is no hope of forgiveness for these people because they have revealed secrets that should have remained hidden. Their punishment is final.

But you, my son, are different. The Lord of Spirits knows that you are pure and innocent in all of this. He has chosen you to stand among the holy and has promised to keep you safe along with those who remain on earth. He has also blessed your descendants, setting them apart for greatness. From your family will come a countless number of righteous and holy people who will live forever."

Chapter LXV

After that, I saw the angels of punishment, ready to unleash the waters hidden beneath the earth. These waters had been prepared to bring destruction and judgment upon all the people living on the earth.

But then, the Lord of Spirits gave a command to the angels who were about to release the waters. He told them to hold the waters back and not let them rise. These angels were in charge of controlling the forces of the waters, and they obeyed His command.

After witnessing this, I left the presence of Enoch.

Chapter LXVI

During that time, God spoke to me, saying, "Noah, I have seen your life, and you are blameless. You live with love and honesty, and I have chosen you for something great.

Right now, the angels are building a wooden vessel. When it is finished, I will protect it with My hand. This vessel will carry the seed of life, and through it, a new beginning will come. The earth will not remain empty. I will make sure your descendants live before Me forever. They will spread across the land and will not be wiped out. They will be blessed and grow in My name."

Then He spoke about the angels who had done evil, saying, "These angels will be locked away in the burning valley your grandfather Enoch showed you. It is in the west, among the mountains of gold, silver, iron, soft metal, and tin.

I saw that valley trembling violently, shaking with molten fire and rushing water. A terrible smell of sulfur came from the burning metals and boiling waters. That is the valley where the angels who misled humanity are being punished, trapped beneath the earth. Rivers of fire flow through those valleys, where these angels suffer for the harm they caused to the people of the earth.

In those days, the waters of that place will have two effects. For the kings, the powerful, and the rulers of the earth, these waters will heal their bodies. But for their spirits, these same waters will bring punishment, because their hearts are full of greed and desire. Even as they suffer and see their own judgment, they will still refuse to believe in My name.

As their physical pain increases, their spirits will also change, and their punishment will last forever. No one will be able to speak empty words or make excuses before Me, because judgment will come to them. This will happen because they trusted in their own selfish desires and rejected the Spirit of the Lord.

Even the waters themselves will change during those days. When the angels are being punished, the springs will turn burning hot, like fire. And when the angels rise from them, the waters will suddenly become freezing cold.

Then I heard Michael say, "This punishment of the angels is a warning to the kings and rulers of the earth. These waters, which they use for healing and pleasure, will not help them see the truth. They will not understand that one day, these waters will turn into an eternal fire that will consume them forever."

Chapter LXVII

After that, my grandfather Enoch taught me everything written in the Book of Parables. These were the secrets revealed to him, and he carefully arranged them for me to understand.

On that day, Michael spoke to Raphael, saying, "The power of these revelations is overwhelming, and it makes me tremble. The judgment written in these secrets is so severe, especially the punishment of the fallen angels. How can anyone endure such a harsh judgment, where they completely perish?"

Michael continued, "Who could listen to these words and not be deeply affected? Who wouldn't feel troubled after hearing this sentence against them, knowing how they led so many others astray?"

Then, as Michael stood before the Lord of Spirits, he spoke to Raphael again, "I cannot plead for them before the Lord. His anger against them is justified, because they acted as if they were rulers themselves. Now, everything that was once hidden will be exposed, and this judgment will fall upon them forever.

No angel or human will share in this punishment—it is theirs alone to bear, and their sentence will never end."

Chapter LXVIII

After this judgment, fear and trembling will overwhelm those who revealed these secrets to the people on earth. The names of the angels involved are: Samjâzâ, Artâqîfâ, Armên, Kôkabêl, Tûrâêl, Rûmjâl, Dânjâl, Nêqâêl, Barâqêl, Azâzêl, Armârôs, Batarjâl, Busasêjal, Hanânêl, Tûrêl, Sîmâpêsîêl, Jetrêl, Tûmâêl, Tûrêl, Rumâêl, and Azâzêl. Each of them was a leader, commanding groups of angels in different ranks.

The first angel, Jeqôn, led the sons of God away from their heavenly place, bringing them down to earth and tempting them with human women. The second, Asbeêl, convinced them to disobey by misleading them into impurity. The third, Gâdreêl, introduced weapons and tools of war to humanity, teaching them how to make shields, armor, swords, and other deadly instruments. From that moment on, people began to fight and harm each other.

The fourth angel, Pênêmûe, taught people the difference between sweet and bitter, as well as the hidden secrets of wisdom. He also introduced writing and the use of ink and paper. Because of this knowledge, many have fallen into sin, and this influence continues to this day. Humanity was not originally meant to live this way. They were supposed to remain pure and free from death, but their desire for knowledge led to their downfall.

The fifth angel, Kâsdejâ, revealed dark secrets about spirits, demons, and harmful influences. He taught people about things like the destruction of unborn babies, snake bites, and the dangers of the sun's heat. He also introduced them to Tabââ'ĕt, the son of the serpent, and many other afflictions.

Another angel, Kâsbeêl, was once highly honored and lived in great glory above. He sought to learn the hidden name of power from Michael so he could use it in an oath that would strike fear into those who spread forbidden knowledge to humanity. This oath was so powerful that it held the heavens and the earth together. Michael was entrusted with this sacred oath, called Akâe.

This oath is incredibly strong. It has supported the heavens since the beginning of creation and will continue to do so forever. Through this oath, the earth was set in place upon the waters, and streams flow from the hidden parts of the mountains, remaining constant from the beginning of time. It also controls the sea, keeping it within its boundaries of sand, preventing it from flooding the land. This command has existed since the world was made and will never be broken.

Because of this oath, the deep foundations of the earth remain unshaken forever. The same oath also keeps the sun and moon on their paths, making sure they continue their cycles without fail. The stars follow this oath as well, staying in their assigned places and responding when called by name. They remain faithful forever.

This same oath guides the movement of the winds, the waters, and the breezes from all directions. It also controls the sounds of thunder, the flashes of lightning, and the storehouses of hail, frost, mist, rain, and dew. These forces of nature praise and honor the Lord of Spirits with all their strength, and their very existence is an act of gratitude. They rejoice and give glory as they celebrate the name of the Son of Man.

The Son of Man sat on the throne of glory, and the power to judge was given to him. He declared the removal and destruction of sinners and those who misled others. They were bound in chains and thrown into a place of ruin, erased from the earth. From that moment on, corruption was no more.

For the Son of Man had arrived and taken his place on the throne of glory. All evil disappeared from his presence. His word went out with power, standing firm before the Lord of Spirits. From that day forward, righteousness and peace would last forever.

Third Parable of Enoch

Chapter LXIX

During his life, his name was honored and recognized before the Son of Man and the Lord of Spirits among the people on earth. Then, he was taken away on chariots of the spirit, and his name was no longer mentioned among them. From that moment on, I was no longer counted as one of them.

Instead, I was placed between two winds, the North and the West, where angels arrived with measuring cords to prepare a place for the chosen and the righteous.

In that place, I saw the first ancestors and the righteous ones who had lived there since the beginning of time.

Chapter LXX

After this, my spirit was taken up into the heavens. There, I saw the holy sons of God walking among flames of fire. Their clothes were shining white, and their faces glowed as brightly as fresh snow.

I saw two streams of fire that sparkled with a beautiful blue glow, like the color of a hyacinth. Overwhelmed by awe, I fell face down before the Lord of Spirits. Then, the archangel Michael came to me, took my right hand, and helped me up. He led me deep into the mysteries of heaven and revealed to me the hidden secrets of righteousness.

Michael showed me the farthest reaches of heaven, the chambers of the stars, and the sources of the heavenly lights, explaining how they shine before the holy ones. Then, he carried my spirit even higher, to the highest heaven. There, I saw something like a magnificent structure made of shining crystals. Between the crystals, flames of living fire flickered and danced.

I saw a great belt of fire surrounding this house of glory, with streams of fire flowing on all four sides. Around it stood the Seraphim, Cherubim, and Ophanim, heavenly beings that never sleep and always guard the throne of glory.

There were countless angels, more than I could ever count—thousands upon thousands, and ten thousand times ten thousand—all gathered around this place. Among them were Michael, Raphael, Gabriel, and Phanuel, along with many other holy angels, entering and leaving this glorious dwelling.

Then, I saw the Ancient One Himself. His hair was white as wool, and His clothes shone with a brightness beyond words.

When I saw Him, I fell to the ground, completely overwhelmed. My body lost all strength, and my spirit was changed. Filled with the power of the Spirit, I cried out in a loud voice, blessing, glorifying, and praising the Lord of Spirits.

The words of praise that came from my mouth pleased the Ancient One. Then, He appeared with Michael, Gabriel, Raphael, and Phanuel, along with countless angels shining in their heavenly glory.

Part of what I saw was beyond my understanding. It spoke of the Son of Man, who stood beside the Ancient One.

One of the angels came to me, greeted me warmly, and explained the vision. He said, "This is the Son of Man, who was born in righteousness. He carries the righteousness of the Ancient One, and it will never leave Him."

The angel continued, "He brings peace to you in the name of the world to come. From the beginning of time, peace has flowed from Him, and it will remain with you forever. All will follow His ways, for righteousness will never depart from Him. He will live among His people, and they will belong to Him forever. They will never be separated from Him, for all eternity."

The angel finished by saying, "In this Son of Man, there will be endless life. The righteous will have peace and live in goodness, always in the name of the Lord of Spirits, forever and ever."

Thank You for Reading

Dear Reader,

We hope this timeless classic has sparked your imagination and enriched your literary journey. Now that you've turned the final page, we want to share a vision for the future of reading—one where every classic you've ever wanted to explore is at your fingertips, in a format that best suits your life.

We'd like to invite you to gain immediate, unlimited digital & audiobook access to hundreds of the most treasured literary classics ever written—along with the option to secure deluxe paperback, hardcover & box set editions at printing cost. Together, we can spark a new global literary renaissance alongside our small, independent publishing house called "The Library of Alexandria."

Thousands of years ago, the Library of Alexandria stood as a beacon of knowledge—until it was lost to history. We aim to reignite that spirit of preservation and discovery right now, in the modern age—only this time, it's accessible to all, in every language and every format.

Picture a world where every timeless classic, novel, poem, or philosophical treatise is not only available to read but also updated for today's readers—modernized, translated into any language or dialect, and ready to enjoy in any format you choose, whether that is in an eBook, audiobook, paperback, or deluxe hardcover & box set version a printing cost.

By joining our movement to rebuild the modern Library of Alexandria, you become part of an unprecedented mission to offer:

- **Unlimited Audiobook & eBook Access to the Greatest Classics of All Time**

  Instantly explore thousands of legendary works, from Plato and Shakespeare to Jane Austen and Leo Tolstoy. All are instantly ready to read or listen to, giving you a complete literary universe at your fingertips.

- **Paperback & Deluxe Editions at Printing Costs:**

  Purchase any title in a paperback, deluxe hardbound, or deluxe boxset edition at printing costs, shipped right to your doorstep. Curate your personal library of Alexandria with editions worthy of display— crafted to last, designed to captivate, and delivered straight to your door.

- **Modern translations for Contemporary Readers in all languages and dialects**

  Discover a vast selection of classics reimagined in clear, current language—no more struggling with outdated phrases or obscure references. Next to the original versions, we aim to offer translations in as many languages and dialects as possible.

  As we continue our translation efforts and add new languages, readers everywhere can connect with these works as if they were written today. By bridging linguistic divides, you're contributing to ensuring that these timeless stories become more meaningful, accessible, and inspiring for people across the globe.

- **Your Personal Library of Alexandria:**

  Over the months and years, you'll curate a unique physical archive of classics—each volume a testament to your taste, curiosity, and love of knowledge. It's not just about owning books—it's about curating a cultural legacy you'll cherish and pass down for generations to come.

- **Join a Global Literary Renaissance:**

  Your support fuels an ongoing mission: allowing us to reinvest in offering deluxe print editions (including special boxsets) at their true cost, broaden the range of available formats and translations, and extend the reach of these works to new audiences worldwide. By joining today, you're not just preserving a legacy of masterpieces; you set in motion a powerful wave of literary accessibility.

We are more than a publisher—we're a movement, and we can't do it alone. Your support lets us scale our mission, preserving and reimagining history's greatest works for tomorrow's readers.

Become a Torchbearer of knowledge.

Thank you for picking up this book and allowing us into your literary journey. As you turn the pages, know that you're part of something larger: a global effort to keep these stories alive, share their wisdom across borders and generations, and spark a true cultural revival for the modern era.

If this resonates with you—please consider taking the next step by visiting:

www.libraryofalexandria.com

With gratitude and a shared love of knowledge,

The Modern Library of Alexandria Team

Visit:

www.libraryofalexandria.com

Or scan the code below:

www.ingramcontent.com/pod-product-compliance
Lightning Source LLC
Chambersburg PA
CBHW010732270326
41934CB00016B/3456